A STORY OF LIFE AT WOLFE RANCH

by Maxine Newell

CANYONLANDS NATURAL HISTORY ASSOCIATION

Delicate Arch, 1906, photograph by Flora Stanley.

Introduction

The historic Wolfe Ranch, located near the trail to Delicate Arch, is a spot that is popular with Arches National Park visitors. Over the years, it has been used as an interpretive tool for providing insight into conditions of early day settlement in southeastern Utah. While the homestead site no longer contains many of the features such as a corn crib, outhouse, and implements, which were used by the earlier residents, there remains much to impart the general feeling of isolation and subsistence farming that it represents.

A Story of Life at Wolfe Ranch is not intended to be a thoroughly historic account of life at Wolfe Ranch. However, it does serve to answer the sorts of questions about what life here must have been like, that often arise in the minds of visitors to this place. With information gathered through personal interviews, researching of public records and other sources, the author has woven a story (told from the perspective of John Wesley Wolfe's granddaughter) that will transport visitors—particularly the younger ones—back to the period of time when John Wesley Wolfe and his family made this place their home.

After Wolfe left the ranch in 1910, it was owned by several others. However, Wolfe and his son Fred, and daughter and son-in-law, Flora and Ed Stanley, "gave the ranch its history," and the marks they left on the land here are the ones that created the memories.

John Wesley Wolfe

A Story of Life at Wolfe Ranch

Esther Stanley sat at her kitchen table in Columbus, Ohio, idly stirring her bowl of breakfast porridge. She wasn't hungry. She knew she must finish her cereal before she left the table, but she was in no hurry. It was summer, school was out, and a long, unplanned day stretched before her.

Her brother, Ferol, had already eaten his breakfast and was outside in the blacksmith shop with their father. Esther could hear the melodious clang of the anvil, and she envisioned Ferol sitting nearby watching the sparks fly.

Thoughts of the blacksmith shop spurred her interest in the day. Quickly she scooped up a few more bites, thinking she'd join her brother. Perhaps Father would pound out a toy for them, if he wasn't too busy. Sometimes he did. Once he made a little wagon, with wheels that turned, and they pulled each other around the yard. But Esther suddenly remembered that her father had promised to repair the neighbor's buggy and, knowing there would be no time for toy making today, she quickly lost interest in the shop.

Again she stopped eating and turned to watch her mother knead bread. Baking day was one of Esther's favorites. Usually Mother gave her a chunk of dough to mold into tiny loaves. After she baked her bread, she sometimes invited Ferol to a tea party. He was not much fun at tea, though. He was only five, and he wolfed down the miniature loaves a whole one at a time! Esther stirred her porridge and decided not to invite her brother. She would just have her dolls.

The little girl's daydreams were interrupted then by her mother's command to, "Listen for the mailman, Esther," and Esther transferred her attention to the door. Today she would beat Ferol to the mail!

The postman's daily visit was an exciting event in the children's lives – especially when he delivered new mail

1

order catalogues. They leafed through the books, page by page, selecting clothes they knew they could not have, or perhaps furnishings for imaginary houses. In the fall, of course, they chose toys for their letters to Santa Claus.

Occasionally, the postman's mailbag contained a letter from Grandpa John Wesley Wolfe and Uncle Fred, away out West, in Utah.

Esther had never seen her Grandpa Wolfe. Even her mother couldn't remember him too well, for it had been years since he left Ohio. Mrs. Stanley often talked about her father, however, and told Esther and Ferol about her own young life.

Esther listened intently as her mother repeated the stories. In time she constructed such a vivid image of her grandfather, she felt she actually knew him: "Your Grandpa Wolfe was a big man," Mrs. Stanley's story began, "so very tall he had to stoop to get through a door. Often, after he closed his butchering shop in Etna for the day, he gathered the four of us about him and sang songs of the Civil War years."

Esther knew her grandfather had been in that terrible war between the States. He had joined the 17th Ohio Battery and fought on the side of the North, even though he was born in Tennessee. Esther decided he must be a very kind man, indeed, to leave his own home to help free the slaves.

Grandpa had fought in several Civil War battles without being wounded. Esther knew them all by heart. He fought at Chicasaw Bayou, Arkansas Post, Port Gibson, Champions Hill, and Black River Bridge. Then, during the Siege of Vicksburg, he injured his leg lifting a big gun out of the mire. After that, he could fight no more. He was given a disability discharge, and he never walked again without the aid of a crutch.

Grandpa Wolfe returned to Ohio and built a home in Etna. Esther sometimes visited Grandma Wolfe in their tall, two-story house. Grandma Wolfe had a big garden and lots of good things to eat in her cellar. Esther thought Grandpa Wolfe must miss his home very much. But, of course, he couldn't come back because of his bad leg. It was much less painful in the West.

Mrs. Stanley always grew sad when she talked to her children about her father leaving: "Your Grandma Wolfe refused to go with him," she explained. "She didn't want to leave her church, and she considered the West wild and untamed, and no place to rear us children."

And so, the family separated. Only Uncle Fred, Mrs. Stanley's adventuresome brother, moved west with his father.

Grandpa Wolfe hoped his family might join him as soon as he was established, but his letters only made his wife more determined to stay in Ohio:

We have started a cattle spread in the Utah desert . . . we call it the $\overline{DX}$ (pronounced Bar DX). Fred and I live in a little log house on the bank of a wash that is sometimes dry, sometimes flooded from bank to bank with roaring muddy water.

We are surrounded with rocks – gigantic red-rock formations, massive arches and weird figures, the like of which you've never seen . . .

But Grandpa's descriptions of the desert climate were less appealing:

The desert is hot in summer, cold in winter. The air is so dry, your lips parch. Sometimes a sudden sand storm threatens to blow our cabin down. But you should see it when it does rain! Waterfalls pour off every cliff. It is a sight to behold!

It is quiet and peaceful here, Grandpa Wolfe's letter continued. *The $\overline{DX}$ Ranch is a day's ride from the nearest store.*

That was enough for Grandma Wolfe. Never, she vowed, never would she move her children to that isolated, primitive land!

Grandpa Wolfe promised to return to Etna the first fall his cattle sales netted good money, but his family knew he would not stay long if he came. He loved the West, and his leg had apparently improved in the arid climate.

"Eventually, I grew accustomed to having my father away from home," Esther's mother concluded her story. "But I never ceased to be lonely for my brother, Fred."

Then Esther imagined her own father and brother leaving her, and she, too, felt sad.

Esther mulled the story of her Grandpa Wolfe as she nibbled at her breakfast. She considered asking her

John W. Wolfe, his wife, Lydia, and two of their children in Ohio.

mother to tell it again, but just then a familiar commotion outside announced the mailman's arrival. The dog was barking, the postman was shouting, "Down, Rover!" and Esther shoved her porridge aside and ran outside to get the mail.

It was a good day. They did have a letter! Even at age seven, Esther could read enough to know it was from Grandpa Wolfe. She rushed into the house waving the envelope.

"Read it, Mother, it's a letter from Grandpa Wolfe!"

Esther's mother stopped kneading the bread and wiped the flour from her hands. Holding the envelope to the window so she would not spoil the contents, she tore open the end and pulled out the letter. A piece of paper fluttered to the floor, and she stooped to pick it up.

"What is it, Mother?" Esther asked impatiently. "Read the letter!"

Mrs. Stanley studied the paper she had retrieved. "Why, it's a postal money order. For a lot of money! Whatever is it for?"

"Read the letter, Mother," Esther prompted again. Slowly Mrs. Stanley unfolded the pages and began to read:

My dear Daughter:

It has been a very long time since I last saw you. Now you are married and have a daughter and son of your own. How I would like to see my grandchildren, for I am growing old. But I cannot return to Ohio. The $\overline{DX}$ is doing well enough — Fred and I raise what we need to eat and sell some cattle each fall. But in this country, if we leave our land unattended for even a month, the cattle will stray away, and the garden will dry up and die.

So, I am enclosing train fare, hoping you will come to see us. You could ride the train to Thompson Springs. There I would meet you with the wagon. Perhaps Ed Stanley, your husband I have never met, could give us a hand on the ranch, and we could all live here together.

The letter was signed: "Your loving father, John Wesley Wolfe."

"What does it mean, Mother?" Esther could barely contain her excitement. "Are we going to visit Grandpa Wolfe?"

"I don't know, Esther," Mrs. Stanley answered. "Run to the blacksmith shop and fetch your father."

Ed Stanley read the letter over and over, stopping between readings to consider the money order.

Esther and Mrs. Stanley waited impatiently for his decision.

"I don't know," he procrastinated. "Utah is a long way from Columbus. Still, you know what they say —

'Go West, young man.' And you can see we aren't getting ahead too fast here."

"We could always come back, if we didn't like it," Mrs. Stanley ventured.

Mr. Stanley caught the wistful tone of his wife's voice, and he suddenly made up his mind. "Of course, you want to visit your absent family. I know how you have longed to see your father and your brother again, and it would be a great experience for the children. And so we will go. Somehow it will work out, or else we will find a way to get back."

Esther jumped up and down and clapped her hands. "We're going out West! We're going out West to see Grandpa Wolfe!"

She rushed outside to be the first to tell Ferol.

A Long Journey

What a long train ride from Columbus, Ohio to Thompson Springs, Utah! Of course, Esther and Ferol enjoyed all three days and nights. They explored the train from diner to caboose and, at least once an hour, they stopped to question their parents: "Are we about there yet?"

Finally, the answer was "yes." The locomotive was screeching to a stop at Thompson Springs. The children squirmed with impatience behind the conductor. From the vestibule, they could see the ground rushing by outside. Slower and slower it moved until, finally, the train clanged, jolted, and groaned to a stop in front of a rough board platform by a tiny railway station.

Esther's heart began to pound. Now she would see her Grandpa John Wesley Wolfe. There he was! That must be her Grandpa! The tall man leaning on a crutch. Grandpa Wolfe was waiting for them!

There were awed greetings, introductions, and handshakes before the Stanleys climbed into Grandpa Wolfe's big four-wheel wagon bound for their new home.

John W. Wolfe's daughter, Flora, her husband, Ed Stanley, and their two children, Esther and Ferol, all dressed up to go out West in 1907.

Mrs. Stanley sat on the springboard, between her husband and her father, while the children rode on a heavy blanket spread on the wooden floor boards of the wagon bed.

"Git-Up," Grandpa Wolfe shouted, flipping the reins, and the harness jingled merrily as the two, big horses trotted down the rutted sand toward the D̄X̄ Ranch, 30 miles away.

Esther and Ferol could scarcely contain their excitement. Now they would see their Grandpa Wolfe's D̄X̄ Ranch.

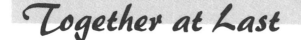

Grandpa Wolfe asked many questions about his family in Ohio, but he took time to describe the countryside as they rode along.

"This is a new world for you," he told his grandchildren. "First, we must cross the desert, and then we will come to the rocks. The gray shrub about us is sagebrush. It is covered with purple blossoms in early spring."

He reached down to pluck a handful of leaves. "Smell," he invited, passing the sage around for all to see. "Crush it in your hands. It smells like the seasoning your Grandmother puts in her Christmas turkey, right? It is good forage for cows in the winter months," he explained.

"Ugh!" Esther exclaimed, making a wry face. She had sampled a sagebrush leaf.

"Silly," said Ferol. "Grandpa just told you it was cow food!"

"Children! Children!" admonished Mrs. Stanley.

Grandpa Wolfe just chuckled. "How good it is to have my grandchildren with me."

"Whoa!" Grandpa Wolfe stopped the horses and, using his crutch for leverage, climbed out of the wagon.

Esther and Ferol watched curiously as he limped through the soft red sand to pick a handful of spindly green spears, joined at intervals like miniature bamboo sticks.

"Here's another plant you don't see in Ohio," he said, handing the leafless stems to his daughter. "Take these home, and I'll brew you a desert drink. It's called Mormon Tea. Good for what ails you when you're sick."

"How much he knows," Esther thought. "How glad I am that we have come to live with Grandpa Wolfe."

"Jump out and walk a ways," Grandpa Wolfe suggested when the children began to squirm on the monotonous ride in the jolting wagon.

Eagerly they obeyed. At first they held tightly to the sideboards of the wagon, until, confident they could explore without being left behind, they darted about, plucking brightly colored flowers which grew along the roadside.

Once Ferol started with fright when he flushed a rabbit from beneath a clump of brush.

"Grandpa! Grandpa!" he cried, rushing for the security of the wagon.

Grandpa Wolfe chuckled. "Why, that's only a jackrabbit, Ferol," he soothed the frightened lad. "He's as harmless ·as your cottontails in Ohio."

Ferol forgot his chagrin when another rabbit took flight across the desert in darting leaps.

"Look at him jump! He's so big!"

Grandpa Wolfe smiled. "What an education these children will get," he told the Stanleys.

Esther and Ferol soon tired of walking and gratefully climbed back into the wagon. Grandpa Wolfe took time to examine the bouquet they had picked.

"Indian paintbrush," he identified some velvety red blossoms.

"And this little purple flower is locoweed. It makes the cattle loco if they eat it!" He pointed a finger to his head and made a circling motion, and the children laughed at his antics.

"Father, look!" Mrs. Stanley had sighted a tall cluster of waxy white yucca blossoms. Grandpa Wolfe turned the horses through the brush and leaned down to break off the stem of white flowers.

"Soapweed," he said, handing the plant to his daughter. He promised to show Mrs. Stanley how to dig the roots and pound them for soap, as the Indians did. "Your hair will feel like so much silk."

At last they reached the red-rock country Grandpa Wolfe had described in his letters. Huge, sculptured formations towered in every direction.

Imaginations ran rampant as the children named the weird features.

"There's a gingerbread boy!" "I can see Cinderella's castle!"

"You haven't seen anything yet," Grandpa Wolfe promised. "Wait until you see the arches!"

A Ranch is Mostly Land

Grandpa Wolfe stopped the wagon on the brink of a hill when they drove within sight of his $\overline{DX}$ lands.

"Where's the ranch? I can't see it," protested Ferol.

Grandpa explained: "Here we don't have big barns and silos, Ferol. In the West, a ranch is mostly land. You can't see much of it at one time."

He pointed to a tiny log cabin that was his home, to a log corral where he kept his horses, and to a winding, green-bordered stream he called "Salt Wash."

"You can throw away your shoes and wade in it every day," he promised the children.

Uncle Fred heard the approaching wagon and rushed down the road to greet them. How they all laughed! A menagerie of animals followed him – bouncing dogs, white chickens flapping their wings – even a horse trotted behind Uncle Fred, anticipating a treat of oats from Grandpa's wagon.

Esther stared in amazement at her Uncle Fred. He was very handsome. But what a surprise to see him so tall! She had expected her mother's brother to be a little boy, Ferol's size.

Esther and Ferol were delighted with Grandpa Wolfe's little log house, perched so precariously on a bank overlooking Salt Wash. A shanty porch protruded from the roof in front, giving the building a fantasy appearance, like a fairy tale illustration.

"Take off your fancy doodads!" Grandpa beamed, as he untied Esther's ribboned bonnet and tossed it upon a high shelf.

But the happiness drained from his face when he turned to take his daughter's hat. Tears streamed down Mrs. Stanley's cheeks. It was obvious that she was disappointed with his home.

"It's not much, is it, Flossie?" he said sadly.

"It's so tiny – and there's no f-floor," Mrs. Stanley sobbed.

Grandpa Wolfe's spirits revived. "Well, is that all that's the matter. So, we will build a new one with bigger walls and a wood floor!"

10

Mrs. Stanley smiled through her tears. What a wonderful father he was! How lucky she was to finally get to know him! She took off her flower and ribbon-trimmed hat and carefully laid it on the shelf beside Esther's.

"Then let's get unpacked," she said bravely. "What are we waiting for!"

And Esther and Ferol, who had already unbuttoned their shoes and discarded their long stockings, bolted down the bank for their first wade in Salt Wash.

Grandpa Wolfe watched and, shortly, burst into hearty laughter. Just as he expected, Esther was stuck up to her knees in quicksand. She would learn to dodge it, but he knew she was in no danger. The quicksand deposits in Salt Wash were not very deep.

Building a New Cabin

What eventful months for Esther and Ferol! They lived in two houses at once. Meals were cooked and served in Grandpa Wolfe's log cabin, but at night the Stanleys slept in a tent.

Everything was exciting to the children, especially building the new cabin. True to his promise, Grandpa Wolfe ordered a wood-floored house for Mrs. Stanley. Uncle Fred and Mr. Stanley dutifully tackled the building project.

Collecting logs for the new house was a tedious job. For months, when time could be spared from the $\overline{\text{DX}}$ chores, the men hitched their horses to huge chains and trailed them to the Grand (Colorado) River, where sturdy trees were plentiful.

After chopping a couple of suitable trees, Mr. Stanley and Fred attached the big chains to the trunks. Then up the wash they dragged them, one log behind each horse, to the site chosen for the new cabin.

The logging days were long and hard, so the children were not permitted to go, of course. They amused themselves at the ranch by climbing up and down the stair-step stack of logs. Higher and higher the pile grew, until, at long last, the men had hauled enough. Then they began cutting them to uniform lengths. With sharp axes they notched the ends, so the corners of the house would be wedged securely.

Esther and Ferol could scarcely contain their excitement when the little house began to take shape. The walls rose fast, and it seemed no time at all before they were working on the roof.

Detail of notched logs.

Never had the children seen a roof like that! A frame of small logs balanced on the log walls and the one gigantic center beam. Over this, the builders spread layers of stringy bark, stripped from the juniper trees. Finally, the insulating bark was covered with gray-green dirt from the nearby hills. When the roof was finished, only the ends of the logs protruded.

The log walls of the cabin were chinked with mud. Esther and Ferol helped, scooping handfuls of the wet clay to stuff into the cracks between the logs, and their little fingerprints were permanently imprinted in the dried clay.

When Grandpa Wolfe was quite satisfied that the new cabin was weatherproof, he directed that the thick pine boards wagoned in from Thompson Springs be laid over the dirt floor. And one fine day, in 1907, the new house was declared completed.

Mr. Stanley ran to the old cabin, picked up his protesting wife and carried her across the threshold of her new home.

Grandpa Wolfe leaned on his crutch and laughed so loud the merry sound echoed through the hills and brought a curious raven circling overhead to investigate the noise.

Grandpa Wolfe was pleased about everything that day – his family, the new house, the wood floor and, yes, even the window. The tiny opening in the new cabin gave the Stanleys a splendid view of his garden. Now they could help shoo the deer out of his vegetable patch.

"Come, Esther! Come, Ferol!" he summoned his grandchildren. "We will go shoot some rabbits for a celebration dinner, while they move the stove from the old cabin to the new one."

Esther and Ferol were always eager for a rabbit hunt. They waited while Grandpa Wolfe tucked his Winchester under his right arm, his crutch under his left, then off they started through the brush. When they were well out of range of the buildings, the hunt began.

Rabbits were plentiful around the $\overline{DX}$, but their gray fur matched the brush so perfectly, the hunters had to watch closely for bobbing white tails. Sometimes Grandpa Wolfe shot a long-eared, long-legged jackrabbit, but these he left on the ground for the buzzards and eagles to eat. He was glad to be rid of the big hares – they were destructive to his garden. But when he aimed his gun at a tender cottontail, the children were allowed to retrieve the kill. His bullets seldom missed their mark. When he had collected six rabbits, he unloaded his gun.

"One more," Ferol invariably begged.

"No more!" Grandpa firmly refused. "Bullets cost money. Waste not, want not!"

At home, the hunters cleaned and washed the rabbits in the trickling waters of Salt Wash. Then Grandpa Wolfe

13

rolled up his sleeves and went to work in the kitchen. He dredged just the legs in flour and fried them in a pan of hot bacon fat. With a flourish, he served his hungry helpers.

Mrs. Stanley turned the remaining rabbit into delicious potpies. Sometimes, after a day of branding cattle, Mr. Stanley and Fred were so hungry they ate a whole potfull.

Mrs. Stanley's Recipe for Rabbit Pot Pie

Soak one or two rabbits in salt water. Wash and drain. Boil until tender in large kettle of water with one cup of chopped bacon. While boiling, drop pot pie squares over rabbit. Boil in open kettle 35 minutes. Stir now and then to keep broth over pot pie.

Pot Pie Squares:

Mix 2 cups flour, 1/2 tsp. salt, 4 tbs. lard, 1 tsp. baking powder, and 1 egg (plus enough water to make 3/4 cup). Mix, roll to 1-inch thick on floured board. Cut in 1-inch squares. Drop over boiling rabbit.

A special footnote to Mrs. Stanley's recipe:

It is correctly printed here. A "potpie" a few generations ago was not the dish that we now call by that name. We suggest that you follow the recipe closely, and then taste the dish you have prepared. After a taste or two, consider the fact that it is quite typical of the foods eaten by settlers and pioneers – and then add whatever you use to flavor stew-like dishes (i.e. salt, pepper). It surprises many people that pioneers ate such bland foods, but salt, spices, and flavorings were expensive and often unavailable.

He Picked the Wildest Horses

Poor Mr. Stanley! He learned the hard way about ranching in the West, from Uncle Fred. The veteran outdoorsman delighted in proving his brother-in-law a tenderfoot. He gave him the wildest horses to ride, then slapped his thigh with glee when Stanley bit the dust. The horses seemed to sense his fear of riding. Even Peg, a gentle horse seven-year-old Esther could ride with ease, bucked when her father climbed into the saddle.

There was no pasture nor winter grain to sustain a milk cow on the $\overline{DX}$, so the family drank canned milk, ordered by the case from Sears. They all adapted except Mr. Stanley. More than anything else at the primitive ranch, he missed fresh milk to drink. He rode the range, watched the wild cows browse, and thought about sweet milk and butter. At last he could no longer stand the temptation. He roped one of the cows, tied her to a corral post, and prepared to milk her. Uncle Fred summoned the family to watch the show.

The wild cow bellowed and snorted a warning, then she hunched her back and kicked both hind feet. Needless to say, the family was back on canned milk.

Uncle Fred slapped his thigh and howled with laughter, of course, but Grandpa Wolfe just shook his head. "I tried to tell that stubborn Scot he couldn't milk a wild cow."

Grandpa Wolfe's pet project was his garden. He worked long hours, hoeing and coaxing water down the long furrows so the gray soil would produce.

Uncle Fred and Mr. Stanley managed the irrigation system – a simple, dirt dam that plugged Salt Wash, captured water in a pond, and spilled into a ditch. The water flowed down the shallow ditch between the two cabins and on to the garden. Grandpa Wolfe hobbled up and down the rows to make sure all his plants got their quota.

Such a garden that was! The parched ground seemed determined to prove it needed only water, and a little help from man, to do its part. It produced giant squash and pumpkins, ears of golden corn, and the sweetest melons ever.

Grandpa stored the melons in the cool root cellar with carrots, pumpkins and cabbages, and, each year, he managed to stash away one melon for a Christmas treat.

Grandpa's root cellar.

Sometimes a cloudburst sent a gully washer roaring down Salt Wash, smashing Grandpa Wolfe's dam. Nothing made him more furious! He ranted and raved and waved his crutch in the air. Uncle Fred and Mr. Stanley jumped into their saddles and rode away until he simmered down.

"He goes on a rampage every time his dam goes out," Uncle Fred explained. "By the time we get back, he will have calmed down, and we will repair the damage. At least the floods do some good. They flush the silt out of the pond."

Grandpa Wolfe's bad leg prevented him from riding horses, so it fell to Uncle Fred and Mr. Stanley to ride the range and check on the $\overline{DX}$ cattle. Uncle Fred was more than happy to oblige. He was an inveterate reader; he read as he rode. Seldom was he seen without a book in his hip pocket and one in his saddle pannier.

Occasionally, the young man rode down Courthouse Wash to Moab to seek companions his own age or to purchase some item needed before the Sears order arrived. Sometimes he took Ferol with him on his spirited steed, but Esther was never permitted to go. Even Mrs. Stanley watched wistfully as they rode away. She had not conversed with a woman since she left Ohio. Once she made the wagon trip to Thompson Springs with Grandpa Wolfe, hoping to see a woman, but there were only men on the street that day.

Prospector and Indian Visitors

Fall was butchering season at the $\overline{DX}$ Ranch. Grandpa Wolfe prepared more than the family needed, so he could feed prospectors and bands of Indians who occasionally stopped to visit and trade.

The butchering process was an interesting diversion for Esther and Ferol, and the fresh beef tasted ever so good after a diet of rabbit, venison and chicken. They especially liked the chewy jerky which they helped Grandpa Wolfe hang on pole racks to dry. The dried meat strips were stored in the root cellar where it was handy for between-meal snacks.

The outdoor life and nourishing home-grown food at the $\overline{DX}$ made the children well and strong. As she watched her happy boy and girl at play, their mother had reason to be grateful that she had not let a tiny log cabin with a dirt floor frighten her away.

Esther and Ferol were curiously fascinated with the prospector and the Indian visitors. The prospectors led long strings of pack burros behind their horses. Occasionally a prospector took time to unhitch a burro for the children to ride. The little animals delighted them so much that Grandpa bought one for their very own.

They named their burro "Jenny," and from that time on, one or both could usually be seen on Jenny's back.

Jenny seemed to sense she was the children's pet. If they were not riding her, she came looking for them, poking her head through the doorway of the cabin to beg for a slice of bread.

Having heard wild stories about the Indians of the West, the children were initially frightened of them. Gradually, however, their fears dissipated, as they discovered the ruddy-skinned people were really very nice, that they were especially kind to children and no different from white men, except they spoke a different language.

The Indians communicated mostly with gestures, but they seemed to think Grandpa Wolfe very funny when he substituted similar hand motions for words. They laughed and chattered in their sing-song language. Eventually, when it was time to leave, they brought forth bright-colored blankets and rugs to trade for meat and garden produce.

The Indians were particularly fond of melon. Grandpa Wolfe anticipated their visits ahead of time, and each spring he planted an extra row of melons in his garden.

Esther, Ferol, and their pet burro, Jenny.

Life at the $\overline{DX}$ agreed with Ferol and Esther.

Every third month, Grandpa Wolfe hitched his horses to the wagon and drove to the railway station at Thompson Springs to pick up the staple groceries ordered from Sears.

He called for his pension check at the Thompson Springs Post Office, mailed Grandma Wolfe some money, and posted a new order for groceries, which Sears would ship in time for his next trip. Grandpa never failed to include a five-pound pail of candy for the children in his Sears order. Their mother carefully rationed the sweets. When there was extra sugar or sorghum, she supplemented the store-bought candy with homemade fudge and toffee.

How the children enjoyed those trips to Thompson Springs! It was a long, hot ride in summer, and so frosty cold in winter that Grandpa Wolfe heated a large stone

19

to place in the wagon bed to warm their feet. On the way home he opened canned tomatoes from the grocery order, and they drank the refreshing juice.

They returned to Wolfe Ranch late at night, long after the children's bedtime. Ferol fell asleep on a pallet of blankets in the wagon bed as it jolted along, but Esther usually stayed awake the whole trip. She rode on the spring seat beside her grandfather, and they talked of many things. Sometimes he told her about his experiences in the Civil War. His leg injury occurred in 1863, while he was on the Greenville Scout in Louisiana. He was helping lift a stalled gun out of the mire when, by a slip, the whole weight of the gun was thrown on him and he was forced downward into the mire. Veins were ruptured in his left ankle. Ulcers developed and spread clear to his hip. At times, he told Esther, while he was in Ohio, he could walk only in a crouched position. Before he left Ohio and moved to the dry West, doctors were talking about amputating his leg.

Grandpa Wolfe still walked with a crutch, but the infection was contained to the leg. He doctored it every night with carbolated Vaseline which he ordered from Sears, Roebuck.

It was quiet and peaceful through the red rocks at night. The only sounds were the jingling and creaking of the harness and wagon, and, sometimes, the echoing yipping of coyotes. Esther cuddled close to her grandfather on the spring wagon seat, even though he assured her the coyotes would do her no harm. They were probably stalking a deer, he said.

Esther's mother always waited up for their return. After the long day's ride, the orange glow of the light through the cabin window was most welcome.

Dining in Style

There was little money at the $\overline{\text{DX}}$ Ranch, but little need for it. Cattle sales in the fall more than covered the cost of grain for the horses and the few supplies needed. Garden produce, wild game, and beef raised on the ranch sustained the family. There was always some money left over from Grandpa Wolfe's $90 quarterly Civil War pension check after the Sears grocery order was posted. This was Grandpa's splurging fund.

He sat in his old wicker rocker on the bank of Salt Wash thumbing through the Sears, Roebuck catalogue, planning surprises for his family.

Once Grandpa Wolfe ordered a camera for Esther's and Ferol's mother. Mrs. Stanley learned to develop pictures herself. At last, she could send photographs of her children to the family back in Ohio.

Mrs. Stanley photographed Esther and Ferol on Jenny the day they rode the steep, slick rock to Delicate Arch. She took a picture of Delicate Arch, of course, and the bench-like formation below the arch which she named "The Settee."

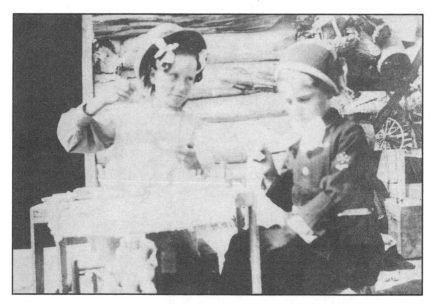

Esther's mud "fudge" looked so good that Ferol tasted it.

Little did Mrs. Stanley know that her photographs, some 70 years later, would end up in the historical archives of the National Park Service.

She captured her children on film at a tea party in front of the new cabin. That was the day Esther fed her brother sand fudge!

Esther was a most proficient mudpie maker. The fudge she molded for her tea party looked so real Ferol actually tasted it, then he cried because it was only sand. Mrs. Stanley felt so sorry for her little boy, she made a batch of real fudge and threatened not to give Esther a taste. In the end, however, she relented, and Esther ate her share of the chocolate candy.

Grandpa's biggest surprise was the 100-piece setting of blue china that he ordered for Mrs. Stanley because she complained about eating off tin plates. When the dishes arrived, he gave all the little butter plates to Esther for play dishes. Then she served her mud delicacies in style.

Grandpa was an Exacting Teacher

Schools were too far away for Esther and Ferol to attend. Grandpa Wolfe filled in as their teacher while they lived at the $\overline{\text{DX}}$ Ranch. Sometimes he held their reading, writing, and arithmetic classes in the log cabin. Sometimes they went for a walk; then the classroom was a big rock warmed by the sun. Or perhaps they hiked to Wolfe Springs, high on the cliffs above the cabin, and there they sat beneath the hanging garden to complete their studies.

When it was time to start down the trail, Grandpa Wolfe filled a big zinc bucket with drinking water from the spring, and the children helped him carry it back to the cabin.

School could be most trying. Grandpa Wolfe was an exacting teacher. Esther and Ferol learned to read and write in both English and Dutch, which Grandpa Wolfe spoke fluently. When lessons were over, however, he moved his old chair to the bank of Salt Wash and, with the children at his feet, sang to them in his strong baritone voice from a medley of old Civil War songs.

Esther and Ferol were growing up. Mr. and Mrs. Stanley were concerned that they had received no formal education since they left Ohio. Esther, particularly, should have some association with girls her own age.

When Esther was ten years old, the Stanleys agreed the time had come to leave the $\overline{\text{DX}}$. They made plans to move to Moab.

It was a sad loss for Grandpa Wolfe. Esther and Ferol had been his constant companions for over two years.

He ordered a new green farm wagon from Sears as a going away present for the family, and he gave them a fine team of horses named Gyp and Peg to pull it. And, of course, the children took Jenny!

The move to Moab was another adventure for the children, but how they hated to leave their Grandpa Wolfe. They had shared many happy months with him on his $\overline{\text{DX}}$ Ranch.

Moab

Moab was but a small village in 1908, yet Esther and Ferol found much to occupy their time. They lived in the oldest house in town, a dirt floor cabin behind the Odd Fellows Hall. But poor Mrs. Stanley! She was back on a dirt floor again and, this time, Grandpa Wolfe was not there to build her a new cabin with a wood floor.

The children made many new friends in Moab, and there was much to keep them occupied. Sometimes, as in Columbus, they walked to their father's blacksmith shop near the courthouse to watch him work with his anvil.

On mail days, the children rushed to the Main Street Post Office after school to watch the stage come in. It was a popular meeting place for the townspeople. They chatted and exchanged gossip, and children made

23

noisy fun while the mail was being sorted, then they took their place in line to collect the family mail.

The most important event of the year was the three day Fourth of July celebration. Mrs. Stanley worked long hours hand-sewing three new dresses for Esther, one for each day of the festival, as was the custom among her friends.

Star Hall

Esther and Ferol lined up in a long queue of children to await their turn for a dipper of lemonade from the wooden barrel on the corner. They watched the horse races in the loose, hot sand of Main Street, and at night they accompanied their parents to a dance in Star Hall, the brand-new community center. When Ferol tired of watching the dancing, he curled up on the benches that lined the walls and fell asleep.

Grandpa Wolfe came all the way from the $\overline{\text{DX}}$ Ranch for the Fourth of July celebration. Grandpa and Uncle Fred had moved into the new cabin, but Grandpa was no longer content to live in isolation, now that the children were gone. When he visited them in town, he took Esther and Ferol fishing in the Grand River. Each time

24

he made the lonely trip back to his ranch, he was more reluctant than ever to leave his grandchildren.

On May 23, 1910, he had one more reason to visit the Stanleys. Esther's and Ferol's sister, Volna, was born. Of course, Grandpa Wolfe made a special trip to Moab to see his new granddaughter.

He never returned to the $\overline{DX}$. He sold the land instead, and in June, 1910, when the Stanleys moved back to Ohio, Grandpa Wolfe and Fred went with them. They were leaving behind many years of good life, but it was time to go home.

As they made their last trip through the red-rock country, Esther and Ferol gazed wistfully at the familiar formations. Four years had gone by since they left Columbus. Esther was but seven years old then. She was now a young lady of eleven. Such impressive years! All her life she would remember and write about the experiences and people she had known. Especially the years at the $\overline{DX}$ Ranch with Grandpa John Wesley Wolfe.

Postscript

In 1971, as Guest of Honor at a ceremony at Wolfe Ranch, Esther Stanley Rison was asked for comments. Mrs. Rison glanced about and said: "It doesn't look the same. Everything's missing."

Yes, Esther, the passing years have brought many changes to Salt Valley. But compare your childhood memories of Grandpa's ranch with the way the area looks today. The rocks and hills and cliffs are little changed. Only man's efforts to alter the scene are proving temporary.

Remember the earthen dam across Salt Wash that stored water for your grandfather's garden? It's gone now. Floods have removed all traces of it. The garden dried up and died, and erosion has eradicated the furrows where melons and pumpkins grew.

The $\overline{\text{DX}}$ cattle would not graze in knee-deep grass today. Overuse of the land has rooted it out. Plants more adapted to the disturbed environment have taken over. Beautiful as they are, dock, locoweed, and evening primrose cannot fatten a herd of cattle. In time, the grasses and other native plants will come back. But it's a slow process.

Your grandfather's old cabin is not here anymore. The new cabin still stands where you and your family lived, mute evidence of time gone by. In 1906 it was erect and weatherproof. Mud that chinked the logs was imprinted with the seven and five year old fingerprints left by you and your brother, Ferol.

Nearby, and quite intact, is the log root cellar where your grandfather stored the groceries he ordered from Sears, Roebuck Mail Order Company. Perhaps some of the blue, mail order dishes lie buried beneath the dunes of sand that have drifted against the walls.

Salt Wash is much different from when you waded in it as a child. The banks have eroded some, and the channel has changed a lot. But it is still an innocent looking, trickling stream. Until it rains! Then it becomes a raging torrent of sand-filled water that cleanses its channel of debris as ferociously as it swept away your grandfather's dam.

Had he been less persistent, John Wesley Wolfe's ranching era would have been considerably shorter.

John Wesley Wolfe's claim to fame is elementary. He was here.

The $\overline{\text{DX}}$ was a lonely, isolated place when Grandpa and Uncle Fred came here. But it did have the bare necessities for ranching – grass and water for cattle, good soil and water for a garden, and a spring to provide drinking water for people. The $\overline{\text{DX}}$ was not destined to greatness as a ranch, however. Its capacity was too limited, its plant life too fragile to tolerate the demands of people.

Still, the land supported Fred and Grandpa for many years, and you, Ferol, and your parents for the last few of those years. People used the land, then and later, drawing from it the means of supporting lives. But we imposed our will upon the land, and it gradually changed. The delicate processes of renewing life faltered, and some of the most useful grasses relinquished their precarious hold on life.

Now, people use the land in other ways, and the native plants are gradually returning. In time, the natural vegetation will recover and, hopefully, many of Grandpa's works will be restored.

And that's what Wolfe Ranch is all about. An historic place in a natural setting. A place where one may visit the past and learn to better understand the present.

Perhaps, if we learn more of the causes and effects of environmental changes we impose upon our world, we can learn to live in harmony with the land that supports us.

Esther Stanley Rison (left) with the Daughters of Utah Pioneers at the dedication of Wolfe Ranch as a National Environmental Study Area on May 18, 1971.

Editors: Diane Allen; Jeanne Treadway
Photographs: National Park Service
Cover design: David Jenney
Production design: Gloria Brown; Workingman's Graphics/Moab
Introduction: Karla Hancock

Published by Canyonlands Natural History Association,
an independent, nonprofit corporation organized to
complement the educational and interpretive programs of
the Bureau of Land Management, the National Park Service,
and the United States Forest Service in Southeastern Utah.

ISBN 978-0-93740-709-7

Canyonlands Natural History Association
3031 So. Hwy 191, Moab, Utah 84532
435-259-6003 www.cnha.org

Fourth printing 2005
Third printing 1995
Second printing 1978
First printing 1974